LUDWIG VAN BEETHOVEN

SYMPHONY No. 3

E♭ major/Es-Dur/Mi♭ majeur
Op. 55
"Eroica"

Edited by
Richard Clarke

T0084451

Ernst Eulenburg Ltd

London · Mainz · Madrid · New York · Paris · Prague · Tokyo · Toronto · Zürich

CONTENTS

BEETHOVEN'S SYMPHONIC PRODUCTION: COMPOSITION, PERFORMANCE, PUBLICATION
BEETHOVENS SINFONISCHES WERK: DATEN DER ENTSTEHUNG, URAUFFÜHRUNG, VERÖFFENTLICHUNG

	Title and key/ Titel und Tonart	(Preliminary) principal dates of composition/ (Entwürfe) Haupt-Kompositionsdaten	First performance (all in Vienna/Uraufführung (alle in Wien)	First edition/Erstausgabe	Dedication/Widmung
Hess 298	*Sinfonia*, C minor/Moll (sketches/Skizzen)	? late 1780s/späte 1780er	–	–	–
–	*Symphony*, C	c. 1795–1797			
Op.21	Symphony No. 1, C	1799–1800	Burgtheater, 2 April 1800	Hoffmeister, Vienna/ Wien, December 1801	Freiherr Gottfried van Swieten
Op.36	Symphony No.2, D	1801–1802	Theater an der Wien, 5 April 1803	Bureau of Arts and Industry, Vienna/Kunst- und Industrie-Kontor, Wien, March/März 1804	Fürst Carl von Lichnowsky
Op.55	Symphony No.3, E♭ (*Sinfonia eroica*)	1803–1804	Theater an der Wien, 7 April 1805	Bureau of Arts and Industry, Vienna/Kunst und Industrie-Kontor, Wien, October 1806	Fürst Franz Joseph von Lobkowitz
Op.60	Symphony No.4, B♭	1806	Palais Lobkowitz 7 March 1807	Bureau of Arts and Industry, Vienna/Kunst und Industrie-Kontor, Wien, 1808	Graf Franz von Oppersdorff
Op.67	Symphony No.5, C minor/Moll	(1804–1805) 1807–1808	Theater an der Wien, 22 December 1808	Breitkopf & Härtel, Leipzig, March/März 1809	Fürst Lobkowitz und Graf Andreas von Rasumovsky
Op.68	Symphony No.6, F (*Sinfonia pastorale*)	(1807) 1808	Theater an der Wien, 22 December 1808	Breitkopf & Härtel, Leipzig, May 1809	Fürst Lobkowitz und Graf Rasumovsky
Op.92	Symphony No.7, A	1811–1812	Great Hall of the University/Universitäts-Aula, 8 December 1813	Steiner, Vienna/Wien November 1816	Graf Moritz von Fries
Op.93	Symphony No.8, F	1812	Großer Redoutensaal, 27 February 1814,	Steiner, Vienna/Wien 1817	–
Op.125	Symphony No.9 D minor/ Moll ('Choral')	(1812–1822) 1823–1824	Kärntnertortheater, 7 May 1824	Schott, Mainz, August 1826	König Friedrich Wilhelm von Preußen

PREFACE

Despite the well-known tradition in Beethoven criticism of assigning the composer's works to one of three creative periods, the nine symphonies are perhaps best divided into four groups. The First and Second were written during the time that conventionally marks the transition between the early and middle period. The next four belong to what may be described as the 'heroic phase',[1] which begins in 1803 and is marked by a prodigious output of highly original works on a grand scale. The Seventh and Eighth, which mark the end of the middle period, show a certain retreat from the bold directions taken in the first six works. The Ninth is Beethoven's only symphony of the last 15 years of his life; and its unusual structure and unprecedented large performing forces place it in a category of its own.

In fact, Symphonies 1 and 2 look back to 18th-century Viennese classicism more than they foreshadow their composer's path-breaking achievements in the genre; the Second, in particular, enjoys a close kinship with Mozart's 'Prague' Symphony (K504) of 1786, a work with which it shares tonality, mood, and the shape of the slow introduction to the first movement. The *Eroica* was begun immediately after the Second, but under profoundly different personal circumstances for its composer: it is the first work in which he came to terms with his increasing deafness by going far beyond the limits of musical convention. The next symphony Beethoven began composing, in C minor (the Fifth), took the genre a stage further by its concern for overall planning, its four contrasting movements being 'unified' by the presence – at different levels – of the parallel tonality of C major. In the *Sinfonia pastorale* (the Sixth) he solved the problem of large-scale organisation in other ways, by joining the last three movements to one another and by drawing a dynamic curve across the entire work.

Beethoven's progress as a symphonist did not pursue a single path, or a straight line, as seems to have been the case in the string quartets. The Fourth Symphony, which was composed quickly in the summer of 1806 and represents something of a return to classical principles (the orchestral forces required for it are the smallest for a Beethoven symphony), may have been released before the Fifth on account of unfavourable reactions to the *Eroica* after its first performance in 1805. It is more likely that memories of the artistic failure of the first concert featuring the Fifth and Sixth Symphonies prompted the composer to write a pair of musically lighter works, or at least cooler ones, in 1811–12; more than the Fourth Symphony, the Eighth marks a return to 18th-century symphonic dimensions.

With the Ninth, of course, Beethoven resumed his pioneering role as a symphonist, combining a supreme command of sonata structures and orchestral technique with masterly control of the additional forces of chorus and solo voices to shape a type of composition hitherto unknown in serious concert music. This fusion of symphony and oratorio was by no means quickly realized. The intention to write a symphony in D minor was first expressed during the composition of the Eighth; the theme of the Scherzo was first sketched a few years later in 1815; the first sketchleaf entry describing a symphony with chorus dates from 1818.[2] By the time the Ninth was completed 12 years had elapsed since the previous symphonies; only the composition of a still more innovatory set of works, the late string quar-

---

[1] The expression was coined by Alan Tyson (in his essay 'Beethoven's Heroic Phase', *The Musical Times*, CX (1969), 139–41) in connection with the years 1803–5, which saw the composition of the *Eroica*, the oratorio *Christus am Ölberge* ('The Mount of Olives'), and the opera *Leonore*; but the period may be extended to include the major instrumental works that followed in their wake.

[2] For a full account of the early plans for Beethoven's last symphony, see Sieghard Brandenburg, 'Die Skizzen zur Neunten Symphonie', *Zu Beethoven* 2, ed. H. Goldschmidt (Berlin, 1984), 88–129

tets, remained to be achieved.

Towards the end of his life Beethoven expressed the desire to write one more symphony. Two of his companions from the late years, Anton Schindler and Karl Holz, claimed that large sections of a 'Tenth Symphony' had been sketched and that the work was complete in the composer's mind; but from the evidence of the surviving manuscripts, it appears that little, if any, progress was made on a new work in the genre.[3]

From the point of view of performance and early reception, it is not the year 1803, but 1807 that marks the dividing line in Beethoven's symphonic output. The first four symphonies were originally intended more for private consumption, being written for and dedicated to their patrons and played mainly in aristocratic circles. The last five symphonies were written specifically for public concerts. The Fifth and Sixth, composed in 1813–14, were heard for the first time in December 1808; the Seventh and Eighth (also composed in rapid succession) at a series of concerts in the winter of 1807–8. For each pair of works, Beethoven composed – nearer the date of the concerts – an occasional piece that would provide a fitting end to a musically arduous programme; the Choral Fantasy in 1808, the 'Battle Symphony' (*Wellingtons Sieg*) in 1813. When the Ninth Symphony was first performed in May 1824, in a programme that included other Viennese Beethoven premières, its own finale provided the rousing conclusion to the concert.

SYMPHONY No. 3

The sketches for a symphony in E flat go back to the year 1802, when Beethoven was nearing completion of the piano sonatas Op. 31 and had just sketched the variation sets in F Op. 34 and in E flat Op. 35 (the '*Eroica*' Variations). As Lewis Lockwood has shown, the new symphony was conceived in four movements, with

an *Adagio* in C major in 6/8, a 'Menuetto serioso' in E flat (with G minor trio section), and a variation-finale similar in design to the Op. 35 set; the first movement would have had a slow introduction in 4/4 time followed by an *Allegro* in 3/4 whose main theme bore a striking resemblance to the *basso del tema* of the contredanse on which the piano variations are based:[4]

A second early attempt at a theme for the *Allegro* comes nearer the triadic design of the final version, yet still resembles the *basso* in its outline:

Between these jottings and the main work on the symphony, the composition of the dramatic oratorio *Christus am Ölberge* intervened. By the time Beethoven returned to the symphony, the idea of a slow introduction had been abandoned and the main motif of the first movement definitively formed:

As Gustav Nottebohm has shown, the new theme and the ideas elaborating or contrasting with it led to a movement – and ultimately an entire work – conceived on a far greater scale than had been previously imagined, let alone

[3] The problems of the 'Tenth' are summarized and discussed by Robert Winter in an essay (in English) entitled 'Noch einmal: wo sind Beethovens Skizzen zur Zehnten Symphonie?', in *Beethoven-Jahrbuch*, X (1977), 531–2

[4] Lewis Lockwood, 'Beethoven's Earliest Sketches for the *Eroica* Symphony', *Musical Quarterly*, LXVII (1981), 457–78. The sketches in question are from p44 of the 'Wielhorsky' Sketchbook in Moscow, which was edited and transcribed by Nathan Fishman as *Kniga eskizov Beethovena za 1802–1803 gody*, 3 vols. (Moscow, 1962).

attempted. From Nottebohm's transcriptions, we can see Beethoven's decisive steps in shaping the first movement in a series of substantial single-line drafts supported by shorter but equally significant alternative sketches for specific passages.[5] The first movement having reached substantial proportions in the sketch book, it became clear to the composer that his ideas for the C major *Adagio* and 'Menuetto serioso' could not support movements of sufficient weight for the work as a whole: thus the *marcia funebre* in C minor, with two contrasting sections; and a powerful scherzo and trio emphasizing, respectively, solo woodwind and horn trio.

The sketches for the *Eroica* were completed by the end of 1803, and Beethoven turned his attention to other projects (including the 'Waldstein' Sonata and the opera *Leonore*). The autograph score of the symphony has never been traced; and although the composer instructed his brother Carl to offer the work to the publishers Breitkopf & Härtel in October, the full score was probably not finished until the following year. Beethoven himself offered the symphony, along with several other works, to the same firm in August 1804; but a fee could not be agreed on. After two years' delay, it was published by the Bureau of Arts and Industry in Vienna.

The symphony was performed in private in the winter of 1804/5, and received its official première on 7 April 1805. The critics found it too long, and not thought out in a unified way; this led Beethoven to insert the following remark in the first violin part of the first edition:

This symphony, being longer than usual, should be played at the beginning of a concert, and soon after an overture, an aria or a concerto; for if it were to be heard too late, it would lose its true desired effect on the listener, who would already have been tired by the preceding performances.[6]

Much has been made of Beethoven's intention to call the symphony *Bonaparte*, in celebration of a Napoleonic spirit that was sweeping Europe and of the democratic reforms instituted in revolutionary France. A well-known anecdote, recounted by Beethoven's pupil Ferdinand Ries, has it that the composer, upon learning that Napoleon had proclaimed himself Emperor, tore up the title-page of the manuscript (on which 'Bonaparte' had been written at the top), exclaiming:

He is nothing more than an ordinary being! Now even he will trample over all human rights, to serve his own vanity; he will now place himself above all others and become a tyrant![7]

The story has been corroborated independently, and its truth is generally accepted. But, as Maynard Solomon has shown, Beethoven's attitude towards Bonaparte had been ambivalent for some time before the composition of the Third Symphony, and remained so for some time after the incident recorded by Ries.[8] Early in 1802 he was invited by the Leipzig publisher F. A. Hoffmeister to compose a sonata celebrating the French Revolution or Napoleon's achievements, but refused on the grounds that Napoleon had betrayed the spirit of the revolution by signing an agreement with the Vatican whereby Catholic worship was reinstated in France. A year later, he thought of dedicating the Third Symphony to Napoleon (this may have been a tactical plan, since at that time he was contemplating moving to Paris). And despite his rage over Napoleon's personal ambitions, he reaffirmed the title of the piece as 'Bonaparte' when he offered the piece to Breitkopf & Härtel on 26 August 1804: the surviving authentic copy of the score,[9] from which the words 'intitolata Bonaparte' have been scratched out, also include the pencil remark – not scratched out – 'geschrieben auf Bonaparte'. The title

---

[5] Gustav Nottebohm, *Ein Skizzenbuch von Beethoven aus dem Jahre 1803* (Leipzig, 1880); Eng. trans. by J. Katz in *Two Beethoven Sketchbooks* (London, 1979)

[6] The original Italian text: 'Questa Sinfonia, essendo scritta apposta più longa delle solite, si deve eseguire più vicino al principio ch'al fine di un Academia e poco doppo un Overtura, un Aria ed un Concerto; accioche, sentita troppo tardi, non perda per l'auditore, già faticato delle precedenti produzioni, il suo proprio, proposto effetto.'

[7] F. G. Wegeler and F. Ries, *Biographische Notizen über Ludwig van Beethoven* (Koblenz, 1838, suppl. 1845), 78

[8] Maynard Solomon, 'Beethoven and Bonaparte', *The Music Review*, XXIX (1968), 96–105; revised as chapter 13 of *Beethoven* (New York, 1977)

[9] This score is in the Gesellschaft der Musikfreunde in Vienna

Sinfonia eroica does not appear until the first edition of October 1806.

Despite an early reception that was – understandably – not completely favourable, the *Eroica* won a number of fervent champions in Beethoven's circle of friends and patrons; the composer himself maintained it to be the best of his symphonies up to the Ninth. In time it grew to become one of the most often discussed and analysed pieces in the symphonic literature. Nottebohm devoted his most detailed sketchbook investigation to the first movement. Schenker's analysis[10] is regarded as a classic essay of its type; Walter Riezler's study of the first movement[11] is much admired for its explanation of motivic detail. Tovey's article 'Sonata Forms' for the 14th edition of the *Encyclopedia Britannica* centres on a phrase-by-phrase analysis of the first movement. For these and many other writers, the *Eroica* marks not only a watershed in Beethoven's career but also an important turning-point in the history of symphonic music.[12]

William Drabkin

---

[10] Heinrich Schenker, 'Beethovens Dritte Sinfonie', *Das Meisterwerk in der Musik*, III (1930), 29–401 plus supplementary graphs

[11] Walter Riezler, *Beethoven* (Zürich, 1936); Eng. trans., (London, 1938), appendix

[12] For a comprehensive survey of the analytical and critical literature, see Lewis Lockwood, ' "Eroica" Perspectives: Strategy and Design in the First Movement', *Beethoven Studies 3*, ed. Alan Tyson (Cambridge, 1982), 85–105.

VORWORT

Obwohl nunmehr traditionell Beethovens Schaffen in drei Perioden eingeteilt wird, ist es wahrscheinlich treffender, die neun Sinfonien in vier Gruppen zu untergliedern. Die erste und zweite Sinfonie entstanden zu einer Zeit, die nach allgemeiner Einschätzung den Übergang zwischen früher und mittlerer Periode darstellt. Die folgenden vier kann man einer „heroischen Phase"[1] zuordnen, die sich, 1803 beginnend, durch eine beachtliche Produktion von in höchstem Maße originären Werken großen Umfangs auszeichnet. Die „Siebte" und „Achte" als Abschluss der mittleren Periode lassen einen gewissen Rückzug von den kühnen Wegen erkennen, die er in den ersten sechs Werken dieser Gattung eingeschlagen hatte. Die „Neunte" ist Beethovens einzige Sinfonie der letzten 15 Lebensjahre; ihre außergewöhnliche Gesamtform und nie vorher dagewesene Aufführungsdauer machen sie zu einem Sonderfall.

Die Sinfonien 1 und 2 sind in der Tat eher eine Rückschau auf die Wiener Klassik des 18. Jahrhunderts, als dass sie die bahnbrechenden Errungenschaften des Komponisten in der Gattung erkennen ließen: Besonders die „Zweite" zeigt eine enge Verwandtschaft mit Mozarts „Prager" Sinfonie KV 504 aus dem Jahre 1786, mit der sie Tonart, Grundstimmung und das Vorhandensein einer langsamen Einleitung zum 1. Satz gemein hat. Die „Eroica" wurde unmittelbar nach der „Zweiten" in Angriff genommen, jedoch unter grundsätzlich veränderten persönlichen Umständen für den Komponisten: Sie war sein erstes Werk, worin er sich mit seiner fortschreitenden Ertaubung arrangierte, indem er die Grenzen der musikalischen Konvention weit hinter sich ließ. Die nächste Sinfonie, die

Beethoven zu komponieren begann, stand in c-Moll (die spätere „Fünfte") und war in Anbetracht der satzübergreifenden Anlage, deren vier kontrastierende Sätze durch die differenzierte Präsenz der gleichnamigen Dur-Tonart C-Dur miteinander verklammert werden, ein großer Schritt in der Weiterentwicklung der Gattung. In der „Sechsten", der *Sinfonia pastorale*, kam Beethoven hinsichtlich der großformatigen Gliederung zu einer ganz anderen Lösung, indem er einerseits die letzten drei Sätze miteinander verband und andererseits das gesamte Werk mit einem wirksamen Gestaltungsbogen überzog.

Beethovens Fortgang als Sinfoniker lässt sich nicht als Einbahnstraße oder als gerade Linie verfolgen, wie es sich für das Streichquartettschaffen anbietet. Die vierte Sinfonie, im Sommer 1806 schnell hingeworfen, scheint zu den Ursprüngen der Klassik zurückzukehren – so ist beispielsweise die Orchesterbesetzung von allen Beethoven-Sinfonien die kleinste – und hat vermutlich aufgrund der mehr als zurückhaltenden Reaktion auf die Uraufführung der „Eroica" (1805) vor ihr den Vorzug der früheren öffentlichen Präsentation erhalten. Noch wahrscheinlicher ist die Annahme, Beethoven habe in Anbetracht des künstlerischen Misserfolgs der Erstaufführung von fünfter und sechster Sinfonie sich dazu veranlasst gesehen, in den Jahren 1811/12 ein Paar von musikalisch unbeschwerteren oder gar zurückhaltenderen Werken zu komponieren; mehr noch als die „Vierte" kehrt schließlich die achte Sinfonie zu der üblichen Ausdehnung einer Sinfonie des 18. Jahrhunderts zurück.

Mit der neunten Sinfonie hatte Beethoven natürlich die Rolle als sinfonischer Vorkämpfer für sich zurückgewonnen, indem er den höchsten Anspruch an Sonatenhauptsatzform und orchestrale Mittel mit meisterhafter Beherrschung des Potentials von Chor und Solostimmen verband und so einen Kompositionstyp

---

[1] Der Ausdruck wurde geprägt von Alan Tyson in seinem Essay „Beethoven's Heroic Phase", in: *The Musical Times*, CX (1969), S. 139–141, mit Bezug auf die Jahre 1803–1805, während derer die „Eroica", das Oratorium *Christus am Ölberg* op. 85 und die Oper *Leonore* komponiert wurden. Doch kann man diese Schaffensperiode ebenso erweitern und die in den folgenden Jahren entstandenen instrumentalen Hauptwerke einbeziehen.

schuf, der bis dahin in der ernsten konzertanten Musik ohnegleichen war. Diese Verquickung von Sinfonie und Oratorium war indes von langer Hand vorbereitet. Erste Anzeichen zur Komposition einer d-Moll-Sinfonie gab es zur Zeit der Niederschrift der „Achten"; das Thema des Scherzos in seiner ursprünglichen Gestalt wurde 1815, wenige Jahre später, skizziert; das erste Skizzenblatt, das den Hinweis auf eine Sinfonie mit Chor enthält, datiert von 1818.[2] Bis zur Vollendung der „Neunten" waren seit den vorangegangenen Sinfonien zwölf Jahre verstrichen, und lediglich eine noch umwälzendere Reihe von Werken harrte ihrer Vollendung: die späten Streichquartette.

Gegen Ende seines Lebens äußerte sich Beethoven über sein Streben nach der Komposition einer weiteren Sinfonie. Zwei seiner Wegbegleiter in den letzten Jahren, Anton Schindler und Karl Holz, stellten die Behauptung auf, dass weite Teile einer zehnten Sinfonie in Skizzen existierten und dass das Werk im Kopf des Komponisten vollständig entworfen worden wäre. Jedoch erscheinen die überlieferten Skizzen vergleichsweise unbedeutend, da sie zu geringe, wenn überhaupt irgendwelche, Fortschritte zur Vollendung eines neuen Werkes in dieser Gattung erkennen lassen.[3]

Aus der Sicht von Aufführung und früher Rezeption markiert nicht das Jahr 1803, sondern 1807 die Trennlinie in Beethovens Schaffen. Die ersten vier Sinfonien waren eigentlich mehr für den privaten Gebrauch bestimmt: für ihre Förderer geschrieben, ihnen gewidmet und vornehmlich in aristokratischen Kreisen aufgeführt. Demgegenüber sollten die letzten fünf Sinfonien ausdrücklich dem breiten Publikum vorgestellt werden. Die 1807/08 komponierten Sinfonien Nr. 5 und 6 erlebten ihre Uraufführung im Dezember 1808, die in ebenfalls rascher

Aufeinanderfolge niedergeschriebenen Sinfonien Nr. 7 und 8 in einer Folge von Konzerten während des Winters 1813/14. Als Ergänzung zu jedem Werkpaar komponierte Beethoven kurz vor der Aufführung ein Gelegenheitswerk, das ein musikalisch anspruchsvolles Programm zu einem quasi versöhnlichen Ende führen sollte: 1808 war es die Chorfantasie op. 80, 1813 die „Schlacht- und Siegessinfonie" (*Wellingtons Sieg oder die Schlacht bei Vittoria*) op. 91. Im Mai 1824, als die neunte Sinfonie neben anderen Wiener Uraufführungen von Werken Beethovens dem Publikum vorgestellt wurde, war es ihr eigenes Finale, das den krönenden Abschluss der Veranstaltung darstellte.

SINFONIE Nr. 3

Die Skizzen zu einer Es-Dur-Sinfonie reichen bis ins Jahr 1802 zurück, als Beethoven die Klaviersonaten op. 31 nahezu vollendet und die Variationen-Zyklen in F-Dur op. 34 und Es-Dur („Eroica-Variationen") op. 35 soeben entworfen hatte. Wie Lewis Lockwood nachgewiesen hat, war die neue Sinfonie auf vier Sätze konzipiert. Ein *Adagio* in C-Dur sollte im 6/8-Takt, ein *Menuetto serioso* mit einem g-Moll-Trio in Es-Dur stehen, und das Variationen-Finale wäre im Typus mit dem von op. 35 zu vergleichen; der erste Satz hätte eine langsame 4/4-Einleitung mit nachfolgendem *Allegro* im 3/4-Takt gehabt, dessen Hauptthema eine verblüffende Ähnlichkeit zu der thematischen Bassstimme des Kontretanzes aufwies, deren Gegenstand die Klaviervariationen sind:[4]

[2] Hinsichtlich einer vollständigen Darstellung der frühen Pläne zu Beethovens letzter Sinfonie vgl. Sieghard Brandenburg, „Die Skizzen zur Neunten Symphonie", in: *Zu Beethoven 2*, hg. v. Harry Goldschmidt, Berlin 1984, S. 88–129.

[3] Die Problematik der „Zehnten" ist aufgeführt und zusammengefasst von Robert Winter in einem in englischer Sprache verfassten und mit „Noch einmal: wo sind Beethovens Skizzen zur Zehnten Symphonie?" betitelten Aufsatz in *Beethoven-Jahrbuch X* (1977), S. 531–552.

[4] Lewis Lockwood, „Beethoven's Earliest Sketches for the *Eroica* Symphony", *Musical Quarterly* LXVII (1981), S. 457–478. Bei den fraglichen Skizzen handelt es sich um die Seite 44 des „Wielhorsky-Skizzenbuches" in Moskau, die in einer Umschrift von Nathan Fishman als *Kniga eskizov Beethovena za 1802–1803 gody*, 3 Bände, Moskau 1962, herausgegeben wurden.

Ein zweiter früher Versuch zu einem *Allegro*-Thema kommt dem dreiteiligen Zuschnitt der endgültigen Version schon näher, ähnelt jedoch in seinen Grundzügen der Bassstimme noch immer:

Zwischen diese Notizen und die Hauptarbeiten an der Sinfonie schob sich die Komposition des dramatischen Oratoriums *Christus am Ölberg*. Als Beethoven sich die Sinfonie wieder vornahm, war die Idee einer langsamen Einleitung verworfen und das Hauptmotiv des ersten Satzes endgültig ausgeformt:

Wie Gustav Nottebohm aufzeigte, hatte das neue Thema und die aus ihm entwickelten bzw. zu ihm kontrastierenden Gedanken einen Satz – und letztendlich ein vollständiges Werk – zur Folge, der auf einem größeren Maßstab gründete, als er zuvor vorstellbar, geschweige denn schon einmal angestrebt war. Nottebohms Transkriptionen verdeutlichen, wie Beethoven mit entschlossenen Schritten den ersten Satz in eine Reihe von gewichtigen einzeiligen Entwürfen aufgliederte, ergänzt von kürzeren, doch nicht minder bedeutsamen Alternativskizzen für bestimmte Passagen.[5] Nachdem der erste Satz im Skizzenbuch ein solch beträchtliches Ausmaß angenommen hatte wurde dem Komponisten deutlich, dass sein Grundmaterial für das C-Dur-*Adagio* und das *Menuetto serioso* keine Basis für gleichgewichtige Sätze innerhalb des Werkganzen darstellten: Aus dieser Erkenntnis heraus entstanden der c-Moll-Trauermarsch mit zwei kontrastierenden Abschnitten und das kraftvolle Scherzo, dessen Trio besonders Holzbläser und das Hörnerterzett hervorhebt.

Die Skizzen zur „Eroica" waren am Ende

des Jahres 1803 abgeschlossen, und Beethoven widmete sich anderen Projekten wie etwa der „Waldstein"-Sonate und seiner Oper *Leonore*. Die autographe Partitur ist spurlos verschwunden, und obwohl der Komponist im Oktober seinen Bruder Carl anwies, das Werk dem Verlagshaus Breitkopf & Härtel anzubieten, war das Manuskript wahrscheinlich erst im Jahr darauf abgeschlossen. Zusammen mit verschiedenen anderen Werken bot Beethoven selbst die Sinfonie demselben Verlag im August 1804 an, doch war es nicht möglich, Einigung über ein Honorar zu erzielen. Mit zweijähriger Verzögerung wurde sie schließlich vom Kunst- und Industrie-Kontor in Wien veröffentlicht.

Die Sinfonie wurde im Winter 1804/05 in privatem Kreis uraufgeführt, die offizielle Premiere erfolgte am 7. April 1805. Die Kritiker fanden sie zu lang, der Zusammenhalt sei zu schwach. Dies gab den Ausschlag dafür, dass Beethoven in die Erstausgabe der Violinstimme die folgende Anmerkung einschrieb:

Da diese Sinfonie länger als gewohnt ist, sollte sie am Anfang eines Konzertes stehen, unmittelbar nach einer Ouvertüre, einer Arie oder einem Instrumentalkonzert, denn wenn sie zu spät dargeboten würde, verlöre sie ihren wahrhaften, angestrebten Eindruck beim Hörer, der vom bis dahin Gehörten bereits ermüdet wäre.[6]

Über Beethovens Absicht, die Sinfonie *Bonaparte* zu nennen, um den über Europa wehenden napoleonischen Geist und die im revolutionären Frankreich durchgeführten demokratischen Reformen zu feiern, ist viel spekuliert worden. Der allseits bekannten, von Beethovens Schüler Ferdinand Ries überlieferten Anekdote zufolge hat der Komponist angesichts der Nachricht, dass Napoleon sich selbst zum Kaiser ausgerufen habe, das Titelblatt der Partitur, worauf obenan „Bonaparte" gestanden hätte, mit dem Ausruf abgerissen:

---

[5] Gustav Nottebohm, *Ein Skizzenbuch von Beethoven aus dem Jahre 1803*, Leipzig 1880.

[6] Der originale italienische Text lautete: 'Questa Sinfonia, essendo scritta apposta più longa delle solite, si deve eseguire più vicino al principio ch'al fine di un Academia e poco doppo un Overtura, un Aria ed un Concerto; acciocke, sentita troppo tardi, non perda per l'auditore, già faticato delle precedenti produzioni, il suo proprio, proposto effetto.'

Ist der auch nicht andres wie ein gewöhnlicher Mensch! Nun wird er auch alle Menschenrechte mit Füßen treten, nur seinem Ehrgeize fröhnen? er wird sich nun höher wie alle andern stellen, ein Tyrann werden![7]

Dieser Bericht wurde von unabhängiger Seite bestätigt; allgemein geht man davon aus, dass er auf Tatsachen beruht. Wie Maynard Solomon indes aufzeigte, war Beethovens Einstellung zu Bonaparte schon einige Zeit vor der Komposition der dritten Sinfonie ambivalent und blieb es auch weiterhin nach dem von Ries überlieferten Zwischenfall.[8] Anfang 1802 erging vom Leipziger Verleger F. A. Hoffmeister die Anregung, eine Sonate auf die Französische Revolution oder Napoleons Großtaten zu schreiben. Beethoven weigerte sich jedoch, da Napoleon den Geist der Revolution veraten hätte, indem er eine Vereinbarung mit dem Vatikan unterzeichnete, nach der der katholische Gottesdienst in Frankreich wieder eingeführt wurde. Ein Jahr darauf beabsichtigte er, die dritte Sinfonie Napoleon zu widmen (vielleicht aus taktischen Gründen, da er zu der Zeit mit dem Gedanken spielte, nach Paris zu übersiedeln). Und trotz seines Zorns über Napoleons persönliche Ambitionen setzte er den Titel des Stückes erneut auf „Bonaparte" fest, als er es am 26. August 1804 Breitkopf & Härtel anbot. Die erhaltene authentische Abschrift der Partitur[9] mit den ausgekratzten Worten „intitolata Bonaparte" weist auch die nicht zugleich entfernte bleistiftgeschriebene Anmerkung auf: „Geschrieben auf Bonaparte". Der Titel *Sinfonia eroica* erscheint erst in der Erstausgabe vom Oktober 1806.

Trotz der ersten, verständlicherweise nicht durchweg positiven Rezensionen schuf sich die „Eroica" unter Beethovens Freunden und Gönnern eine Reihe glühender Verehrer, und der Komponist selbst hielt sie für die beste seiner Sinfonien bis zur „Neunten". Im Laufe der Zeit wurde sie zu einem der am häufigsten besprochenen und analysierten Stücke der sinfonischen Literatur. Nottebohm konzentrierte sich in seinem überaus detaillierten Skizzenuntersuchung im Wesentlichen auf den ersten Satz. Schenkers Analyse[10] gilt auf ihre Art als exemplarisch; Walter Riezlers Studie über den ersten Satz[11] wird wegen der Erläuterung motivischer Einzelheiten geschätzt. Toveys Artikel „Sonata forms" („Formen des Sonatenhauptsatzes") für die 14. Auflage der Encyclopedia Britannica beruht auf einer Phrase für Phrase vorgenommenen Analyse des ersten Satzes. In den Augen dieser Autoren und denen vieler anderer ist die „Eroica" nicht nur ein Scheitelpunkt in Beethovens Karriere, sondern darüber hinaus auch ein bedeutender Wendepunkt in der Geschichte der sinfonischen Musik.[12]

William Drabkin
Übersetzung: Norbert Henning

[7] F. G. Wegeler und F. Ries, *Biographische Notizen über Ludwig van Beethoven*, Coblenz 1838, Ergänzungsband 1845, S. 78.

[8] Maynard Solomon, „Beethoven and Bonaparte", in: *The Music Review* XXIX (1968), S. 96–105; revidiert als Kapitel 13 in *Beethoven*, New York 1977.

[9] Die Partitur befindet sich im Besitz der Gesellschaft der Musikfreunde in Wien.

[10] Heinrich Schenker, „Beethovens Dritte Sinfonie", in: *Das Meisterwerk in der Musik* III (1930), S. 29–101, mit beigefügten Graphiken.

[11] Walter Riezler, *Beethoven*, Zürich 1936.

[12] Zur umfassenden Darstellung der analytischen und kritischen Literatur vgl. Lewis Lockwood, „ ,Eroica' Perspectives: Strategy and Design in the First Movement", in *Beethoven Studies 3*, hg. v. Alan Tyson, Cambridge 1982, S. 85–105.

SYMPHONY No. 3

A sua Altezza Serenissima il Principe di Lobkowitz

Ludwig van Beethoven
(1770–1827)
Op. 55

I. **Allegro con brio** (♩. = 60)

Edited by Richard Clarke
© 2009 Ernst Eulenburg Ltd, London
and Ernst Eulenburg & Co GmbH, Mainz

C

22

II. Marcia funebre

Adagio assai ($\flat$ = 80)

Maggiore

Minore

EE 7201

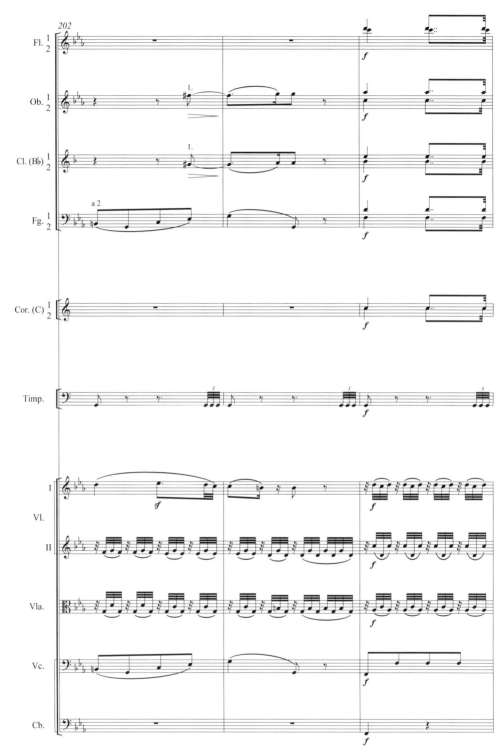

III. Scherzo

Allegro vivace ($\math0. = 116$)

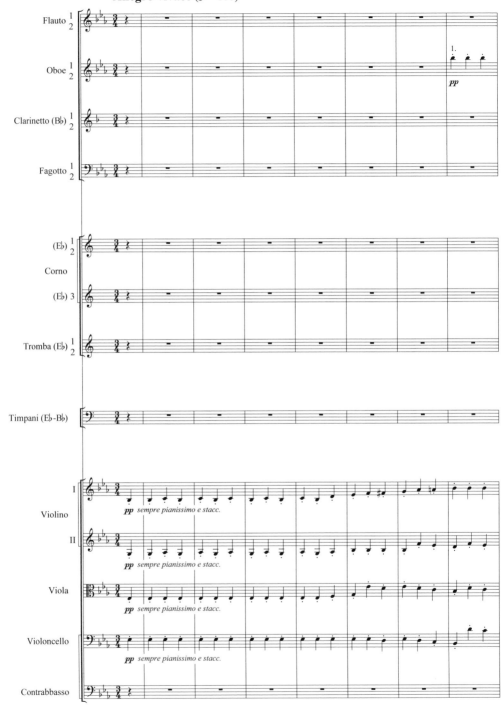

Trio

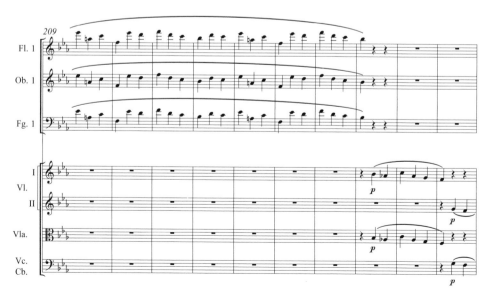

120

EE 7201

Coda

IV. Finale

Allegro molto ($\lozenge$ = 76)

138

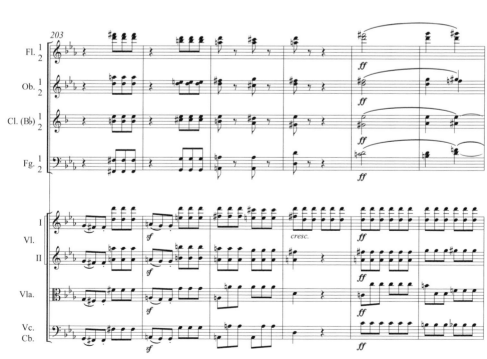

148

Poco Andante ($\eightnote$ = 108)